HARD AS A
Mother

A Guided Journal to Help Moms Thrive in Motherhood

HARD AS A
Mother

Copyright © 2023 by Jackie L. Bobbitt.

No part of this book may be used or reproduced in any manner whatsoever without the prior written permission of the author.

Dedication

I dedicate this book to every mama who is in the thick of motherhood. Truth is: motherhood is hard but you can do hard things. Thank you for trusting me to help you thrive in motherhood.

Love,

Jackie

Introduction

I created this journal to help you process some hard spots in motherhood but to also help you realize how you can do hard things.

While this journal includes some prompts, I have given you plenty of lined pages to express any thoughts you may need to get out of your head and onto paper.

There is no right way to fill in the spaces. I encourage you to pace yourself. Flip through the prompts, respond immediately or come back when you feel ready. Happy Journaling.

Jackie L. Bobbitt

Self-Care

In what ways can you prioritize self-care? What can you do once a week?

_____
_____
_____
_____
_____
_____
_____
_____
_____
_____
_____
_____
_____
_____
_____
_____

motherhood

Is motherhood what you expected it to be? Explain.

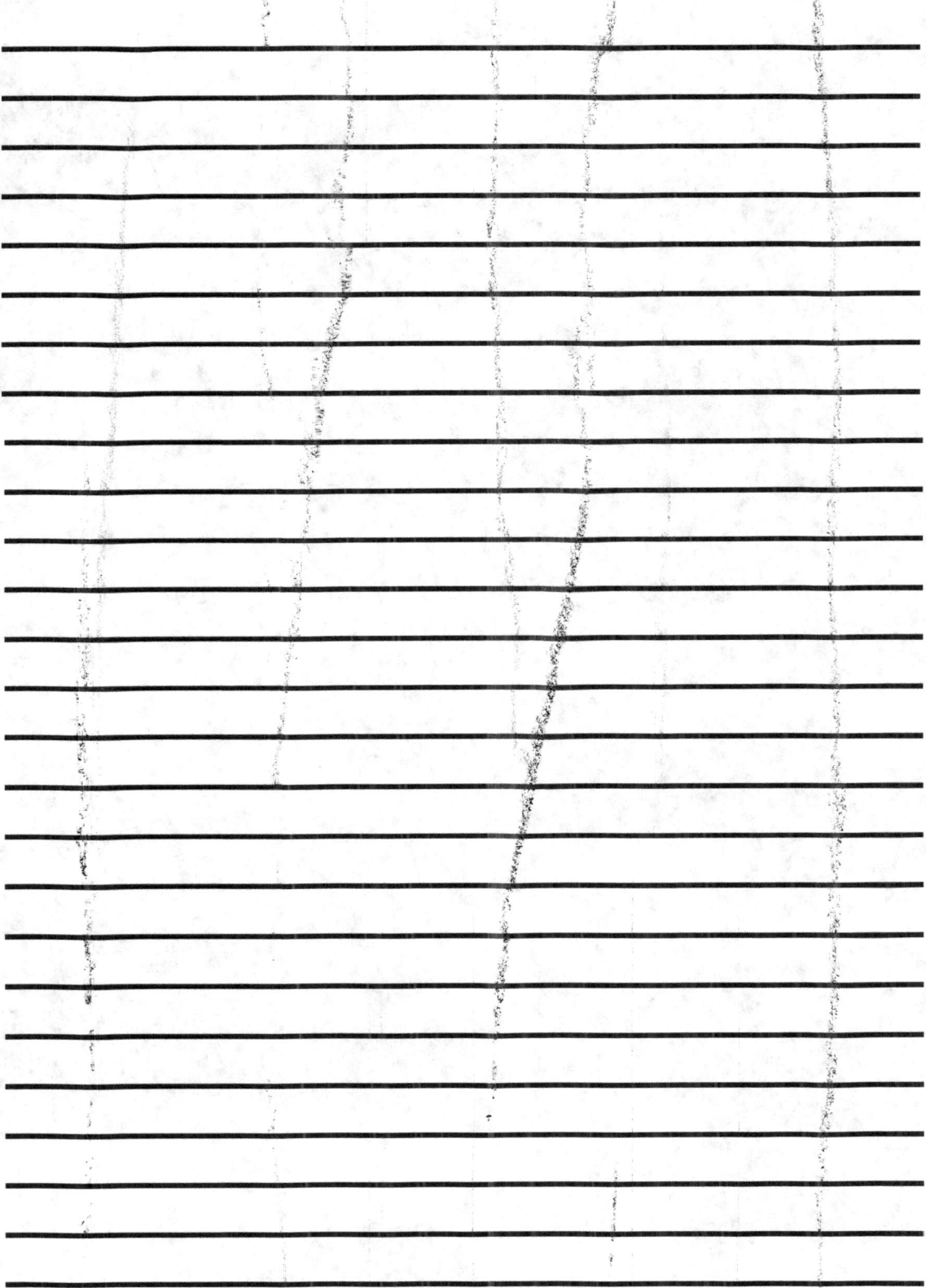

MOTHERHOOD

What are you proud of yourself for?
(Perfect place to brag, mama)

HARD AS A MOTHER

> Describe motherhood in your own (honest) words.

motherhood

Share your experience of "village" as it relates to motherhood.

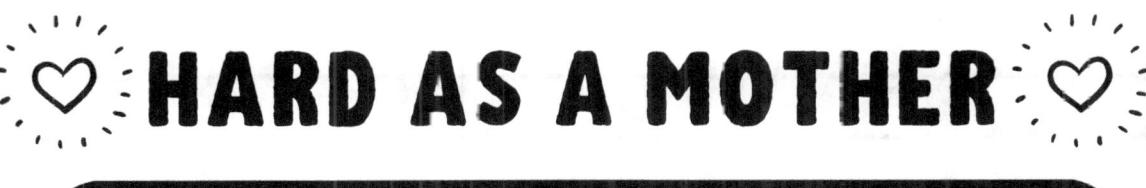

Write down ways you can be more present today.

Self-Care

Have you been pouring from an empty cup this week? Explain.

_____
_____
_____
_____
_____
_____
_____
_____
_____
_____
_____
_____
_____
_____
_____
_____

Self-Care

In what ways can you model self care for your children?

_____
_____
_____
_____
_____
_____
_____
_____
_____
_____
_____
_____
_____
_____
_____

HARD AS A MOTHER

How has motherhood changed you?

Self-Care

Do you feel like self care has to be earned? Why or why not?

_____
_____
_____
_____
_____
_____
_____
_____
_____
_____
_____
_____
_____
_____

Do you find yourself grieving the life you lived before becoming a mom? Explain.

MOTHERHOOD

What do you think your children love most about you?

HARD AS A MOTHER

> What's one task you can do today that would allow you to have a smoother day tomorrow?

Self-Care

In what ways are you tending to your health?

_____
_____
_____
_____
_____
_____
_____
_____
_____
_____
_____
_____
_____
_____
_____
_____

MOTHERHOOD

> What is your purpose? What lights a fire inside of you?

Motherhood is hard but you can do hard things. Give yourself a round of applause, Mama!

Follow me on IG: @thejackiebobbitt
Connect with me via www.jackiebobbitt.com
Subscribe to my podcast on all platforms:
Sincerely, Mama Podcast
Subscribe to my Youtube: @sincerelymamapodcast

www.ingramcontent.com/pod-product-compliance
Lightning Source LLC
Chambersburg PA
CBHW080747060526
44119CB00072B/173